What *Sisters* Teach Us

Happy Birthday
Love you —
Di

What *Sisters* Teach Us

Life's Lessons Learned From Our Sisters

WILLOW CREEK PRESS

Editor: Andrea Donner

Published by Willow Creek Press
P.O. Box 147, Minocqua, Wisconsin 54548

PHOTO CREDITS:
Page 2 © Barbara Peacock/www.barbarapeacock.com; Page 6 © age fotostock/SuperStock; Page 9 © Barbara Peacock/www.barbarapeacock.com; Page 10 © age fotostock/SuperStock; Page 13 © age fotostock/SuperStock; Page 14 © age fotostock/SuperStock; Page 17 © age fotostock/SuperStock; Page 18 © Barbara Peacock/www.barbarapeacock.com; Page 21 © Nicki Pardo/Getty Images, Inc.; Page 22 © age fotostock/SuperStock; Page 25 © Barbara Peacock/www.barbarapeacock.com; Page 26 © Barbara Peacock/www.barbarapeacock.com; Page 29 © age fotostock/SuperStock; Page 30 © age fotostock/SuperStock; Page 33 © Barbara Peacock/www.barbarapeacock.com; Page 34 © iStockphoto.com/Jan Tyler; Page 37 © Barbara Peacock/www.barbarapeacock.com; Page 38 © ullstein-CARO/Bastian/Peter Arnold, Inc.; Page 41 © Barbara Peacock/www.barbarapeacock.com; Page 42 © Nancy Rica Schiff/SuperStock; Page 45 © Barbara Peacock/www.barbarapeacock.com; Page 46 © Barbara Peacock/www.barbarapeacock.com; Page 49 © Barbara Peacock/www.barbarapeacock.com; Page 50 © Barbara Peacock/www.barbarapeacock.com; Page 53 © Barbara Peacock/www.barbara-peacock.com; Page 54 © Barbara Peacock/www.barbarapeacock.com Page 57 © age fotostock/SuperStock; Page 58 © age fotostock/SuperStock; Page 61 © Barbara Peacock/www.barbarapeacock.com; Page 62 © Barbara Peacock/www.barbarapeacock.com; Page 65 © age fotostock/SuperStock; Page 66 © age fotostock/SuperStock; Page 69 © age fotostock/SuperStock; Page 70 © age fotostock/SuperStock; Page 73 © age fotostock/SuperStock; Page 74 © age fotostock/SuperStock; Page 77 © age fotostock/SuperStock; Page 78 © Barbara Peacock/www.barbarapeacock.com; Page 81 © The Copyright Group/SuperStock; Page 82 © Barbara Peacock/www.barbarapeacock.com; Page 85 © Powerstock/SuperStock; Page 86 © Angelo Cavalli/SuperStock; Page 89 © Anton Vengo/SuperStock; Page 90 © The Copyright Group/SuperStock; Page 93 © age fotostock/SuperStock; Page 94 © iStockphoto.com

Printed in Canada

For Deahn and Sarah

Sisterhood is powerful.

Kathie Amatniek

AFFECTION

You know full well as I do the value of sisters' affections:
There is nothing like it in this world.

Charlotte Bronte

*A sister is one who will pick you
up when you are down.*

Unknown

BENEVOLENCE

A sister is more precious than an eye.

Barbara Kingsolver

A sister is a gift to the heart, a friend to the spirit,
a golden thread to the meaning of life.

Isadora James

CAPTIVATION

You don't choose your family.
They are God's gift to you, as you are to them.

Desmond Tutu

Help one another,
is part of the religion of sisterhood.

Louisa May Alcott

CARING

A sister is a friend given by nature.

Legouve

She is your partner in crime, your midnight companion,
someone who knows when you are smiling, even in the dark.

Barbara Alpert

COLLABORATION

More than Santa Claus, your sister knows
when you've been bad and good.

Linda Sunshine

Is solace anywhere more comforting
than that in the arms of a sister.

Alice Walker

COMFORT

A ministering angel shall my sister be.

William Shakespeare

For there is no friend like a sister, in calm or stormy weather,
to cheer one on the tedious way, to fetch one if one goes astray,
to lift one if one totters down, to strengthen whilst one stands.

Christina G. Rossetti

COMPASSION

An older sister is a friend and defender—
a listener, conspirator, a counselor,
and a sharer of delights. And sorrows too.

Pam Brown

If you don't understand how a woman could both
love her sister dearly and want to wring her neck at the
same time, then you were probably an only child.

Linda Sunshine

COMPETITION

Sisters never quite forgive each other for
what happened when they were five.

Pam Brown

We acquire friends and we make enemies,
but our sisters come with the territory.

Evelyn Loeb

COMRADESHIP

Sisterhood is probably the one [relationship] that will
last longer than any other; a sister will always be around.

Jane Dowdeswell

Sisters share their hopes, their fears, their love, everything they have.
Real friendship springs from their special bonds.

Carrie Bagwell

CONFIDANTE

There's a special kind of freedom sisters enjoy.
Freedom to share innermost thoughts, to ask a favor,
to show their true feelings.

Unknown

We don't have to be like one another to enjoy sisterhood.

Barbara W. Winder

DIFFERENCES

A sister is both your mirror and your opposite.

Elizabeth Fishel

My oldest sisters were perfect.
They had perfect hair, perfect everything.

Donna Brazile

EMULATION

My sister taught me everything I need to know,
and she was only in the sixth grade at the time.

Linda Sunshine

She takes my hand and leads me along paths
I would not have dared explore alone.

Maya V. Patel

ENCOURAGEMENT

[Sisters] lived through all your triumphs, all your favorites, all your
loves and losses. They have no delusions. They lived with you too long.
And so, when you achieve some victory, friends are delighted—
but sisters hold your hands in silence and shine with happiness.

Pam Brown

Having a sister is like having a best friend you can't get rid of.
You know whatever you do, they'll still be there.

Amy Li

FRIENDSHIP

I, who have no sisters or brothers, look with some degree of
innocent envy on those who may be said to be born to friends.

James Boswell

A sister is a little bit of childhood
that can never be lost.

Marion C. Garretty

FUN

You can't think how I depend on you, and when
you're not there the color goes out of my life.

Virginia Woolf,
to her sister Vanessa

Sisters examine each other so they can have
a map for how they should behave.

Michael D. Kahn

GOOFINESS

Features alone do not run in the blood;
vices and virtues, genius and folly,
are transmitted through the same sure
but unseen channel.

William Hazlitt

Family faces are magic mirrors. Looking at people who belong to us, we see the past, present and future.

Gail Lumet Buckley

HERITAGE

Children of the same family, the same blood, with the same first associations and habits, have some means of enjoyment in their power, which no subsequent connections can supply…

Jane Austen

*However frank you might think you're being with friends,
honesty reaches a different level between sisters.*

Sandra Deeble

HONESTY

You can kid the world. But not your sister.

Charlotte Gray

She is your mirror, shining back at you
with a world of possibilities.

Barbara Alpert

INSPIRATION

It's very hard in this world to find
someone who can walk in your shoes,
but you come closer to that than anybody.

Corretta Scott King,
to her sister Edythe

One's sister is a part of one's essential self,
an eternal presence of one's heart and soul and memory.

Susan Cabill

INTIMACY

We know one another's faults, virtues, catastrophes,
mortifications, triumphs, rivalries, desires, and how long
we can each hang by our hands to a bar.

Rose Macaulay

Sisters are blossoms in the garden of life.

Unknown

JOY

Today is far from Childhood—
But up and down the hills
I held her hand the tighter—
Which shortened all the miles—

Emily Dickinson

The best thing about having a sister
was that I always had a friend.

Cali Rae Turner

KINDNESS

My sister and me, treasurers of each other's childhoods,
linked by volatile love, best friends who make
other best friends ever so slightly less best.

Patricia Volk

So many shared memories rest between sisters.
Some, like a sleeping grizzly bear, seem best left undisturbed.
While others can fill a rainy afternoon with laughter and sunshine.

Melody Carlson

LAUGHTER

You and I are tied together by years of misunderstandings,
cross words, icy silences, laughter, hugs, tenderness, and love.
All those strands are twisted into a knot
that nothing will ever, ever break.

Ellyn Sanna

To have a loving relationship with a sister is not
simply to have a buddy or a confidante—
it is to have a soul mate for life.

Victoria Secunda

LOVE

I find that as I grow older,
I love those most whom I loved first.

Thomas Jefferson

A loyal sister is worth a thousand friends.

Marian Eigerman

LOYALTY

*Sibling relationships outlast marriages,
survive the death of parents, resurface after
quarrels that would sink any friendship.*

Erica E. Goode

A sister smiles when one tells one's stories—
for she knows where the decoration has been added.

Chris Montaigne

MEMORIES

Only a sister knows about former pimples, failing math,
and underwear kicked under the bed.

Laura Tracy

What's the good news if you haven't
a sister to share it with?

Jenny De Vries

MILESTONES

A sister is sometimes the only person who
sees the horizon from your point of view.

Mia Evans

I would like more sisters, that the taking out of one,
might not leave such stillness.

Emily Dickinson

PLAYFULNESS

Of two sisters one is always the watcher,
one the dancer.

Louise Glück

The bond that joined us lay deeper than outward things;
The rivers of our souls spring from the same well!

Po Chu-I

PRIDE

When sisters stand shoulder to shoulder,
who stands a chance against us?

Pam Brown

The mildest, drowsiest sister has been known
to turn tiger if her sibling is in trouble.

Clara Ortega

PROTECTIVENESS

If catastrophe should strike, sisters are there,
defending you against all comers.

Pam Brown

Big sisters are the crab grass in the lawn of life.

Charles M. Schulz

QUARRELS

Sisterhood...
is a condition people have to work at.

Maya Angelou

There is no substitute for the comfort supplied
by the utterly taken-for-granted relationship.

Iris Murdoch

REASSURANCE

To the outside world we all grow old.
But not to brothers and sisters.
We know each other as we always were.
We live outside the touch of time.

Clara Ortega

Every sister has a fund of embarrassing stories she
can bring out at the most effective moment.

Pamela Dugdale

REMINISCENCES

You keep your past by having sisters.
As you get older, they're the only ones who don't
get bored if you talk about your memories.

Deborah Moggach

With a sister you never have to censor your words.
We talk about everything and nothing.

Sheryl Glass

SENSITIVITY

Sisters touch your heart in ways no other could.

Carrie Bagwell

One of the best things about being an adult
is the realization that you can share with your sister
and still have plenty for yourself.

Betsy Cohen

SHARING

Sisters—
they share the agony and the exhilaration.

Roxanne Brown

We may look old and wise to the outside world,
but to each other, we are still in junior school.

Charlotte Gray

SILLINESS

It's hard to be responsible,
adult and sensible all the time.
How good it is to have a sister
whose heart is as young as your own.

Pam Brown

Sisters are connected throughout their lives by a special bond—
whether they try to ignore it or not.

Brigid McConville

SINCERITY

Sister is probably the most competitive relationship
within the family, but once the sisters are grown,
it becomes the strongest relationship.

Margaret Mead

Sisters function as safety nets in a chaotic
world simply by being there for each other.

Carol Saline

STRENGTH

I can tell you my fears,
which are made lighter by being shared.

Pamela Winterbourne

*There can be no situation in life
in which the conversation of my dear sister
will not administer some comfort to me.*

Lady Mary Worley Montagu

SUPPORT

*Our sisters hold up our mirrors—our images
of who we are and of who we can dare to be.*

Elizabeth Fishel

Sweet is the voice of a sister
in the season of sorrow.

Benjamin Disraeli

SYMPATHY

The only time you look down on me is when
you're picking me up from the floor.

Maria Smedstad

Sisters are inescapably connected,
shaped by the same two parents,
the same trove of memory and experience.

Roxanne Brown

TENDERNESS

A sibling may be the keeper of one's identity,
the only person with the keys to one's unfettered,
more fundamental self.

Marian Sandmaier

How do people make it through life without a sister?

Sara Corpening

THANKFULNESS

Husbands come and go,
children come and eventually they go.
Friends grow up and move away.
But the one thing that's never lost is your sister.

Gail Sheeny

A sister can be seen as someone who is both ourselves and very much not ourselves—a special kind of double.

Toni Morrison

TRADITION

Our brothers and sisters are there with us from the dawn of our personal stories to the inevitable dusk.

Susan Scarf Merrell

A sister's heart is the safest place
to bury all your secrets.

Bonnie Kuchler

TRUST

We are sisters. We will always be sisters.
Our differences may never go away,
but neither, for me, will our song.

Elizabeth Fishel

The desire to be and have a sister...
is a desire to know and be known by someone who
shares blood and body, history and dreams.

Elizabeth Fishel

UNDERSTANDING

Sisters. Yes, we're just sisters.
Our story is not heroic, not even memorable.
But when I need support, I sense you quietly by me.
I always will.

Helen Thomson